IN THE WATER IS WHERE WE'LL BE...

COME VACATION WITH MOLLY AND ME!!

WRITTEN AND ILLUSTRATED

BY CANDY A. JOHANSEN

DEDICATION PAGE

Molly and I would like to dedicate this vacation
book to my brother and sister-in-law, Rod
and Dyanna Lowe and their children, Reed
and Madison. The home we spend our summer
vacations at belongs to them and we're
thrilled to be able to spend quality family time
together in their home and on Beaver Lake.

THANK YOU PAGE

Mom and I (Molly) want to thank Rod and
Dyanna for the use of their home and boat during
our vacation and for their hospitality. We had a
ton of fun. Also, we want to thank the rest of
our family for letting us photograph them so
we could create this vacation book.

ABOUT THIS BOOK

Last summer, my family decided to take a vacation together. My mom's brother and his wife bought a lake house on Beaver Lake in Arkansas. We all decided to spend a week together on the lake. We had a great time. Have you ever taken a vacation with your family? In this book, I'll tell you about my vacation, explain to you why it's important to take vacation and tell you some things to think about when going on vacation.

Taking a vacation means you get to have an adventure.

Have you ever helped your mom or dad pack your bag for vacation?

Me (Molly) and my boy, Jacob

Going *on*
vacation
makes peop*le*
happy!!

Are you happy
when you get
to go on
vacation with
your mom and
dad?

Me (Molly)
and my boy, Jacob

Taking a vacation means you get to travel and see new and exciting places.

Have you ever taken a vacation?

Me (Molly) and *my* mom as we crossed the state line into Arkansas.

WELCOME TO

Arkansas®

THE NATURAL STATE

BUCKLE UP FOR SAFETY

A vacation allows us to spend time at different places, like a vacation home, a motel or a resort

Me (Molly) sitting outside of The Lowe's lake home.

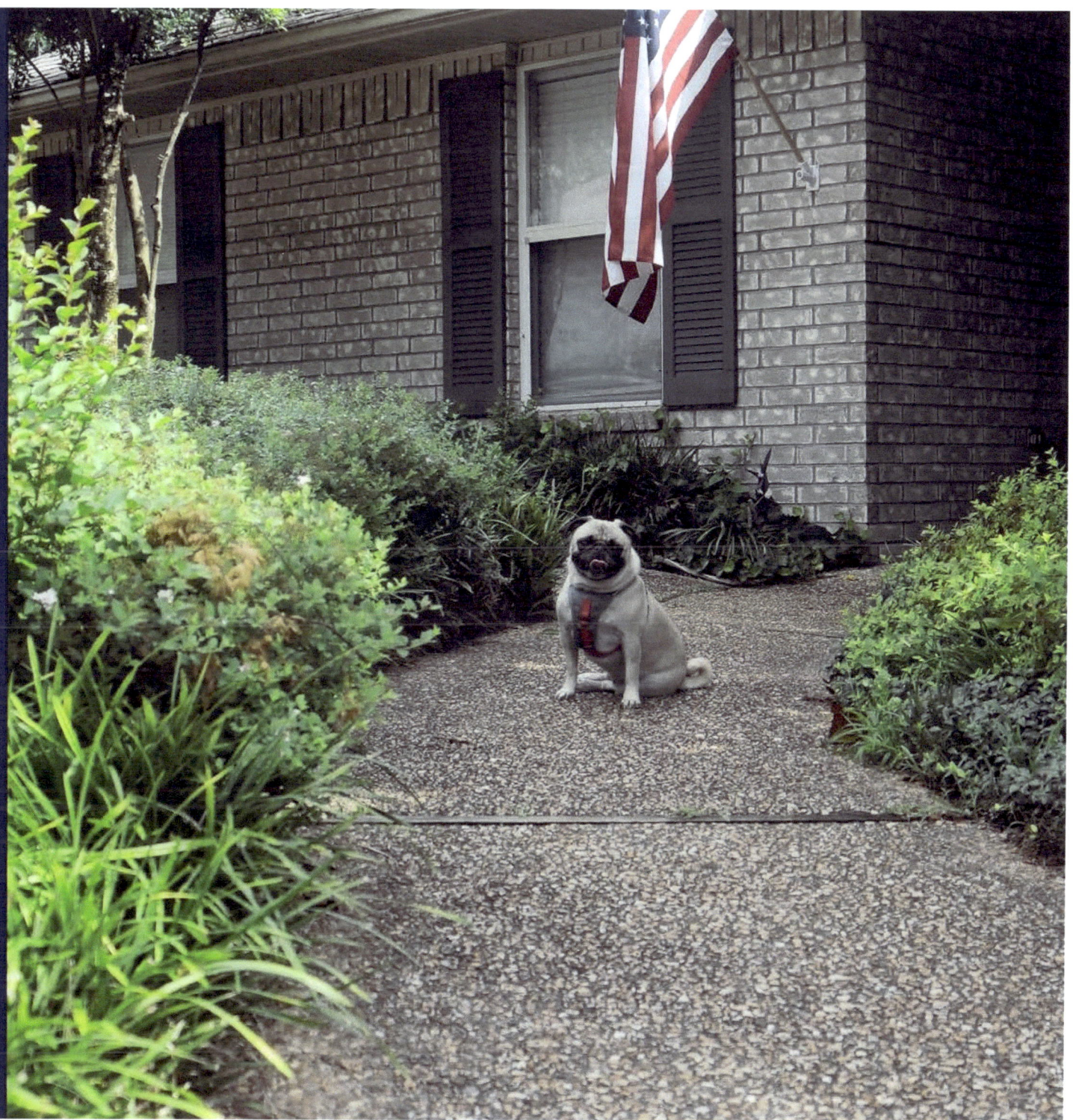

Taking a vacation lets you see the world for yourself.

You might get to see or experience something you learned in school, read about or saw on TV.

Me (Molly) sitting on the front porch of the Lowe's lake house.

A vacation gives *us* a chance to meet new people.

See my face?

These are cousins that I hadn't seen in a long time so I had to get re-aquainted. It turned out great though!!

Me (Molly) with Ashley and Trevin Lowe

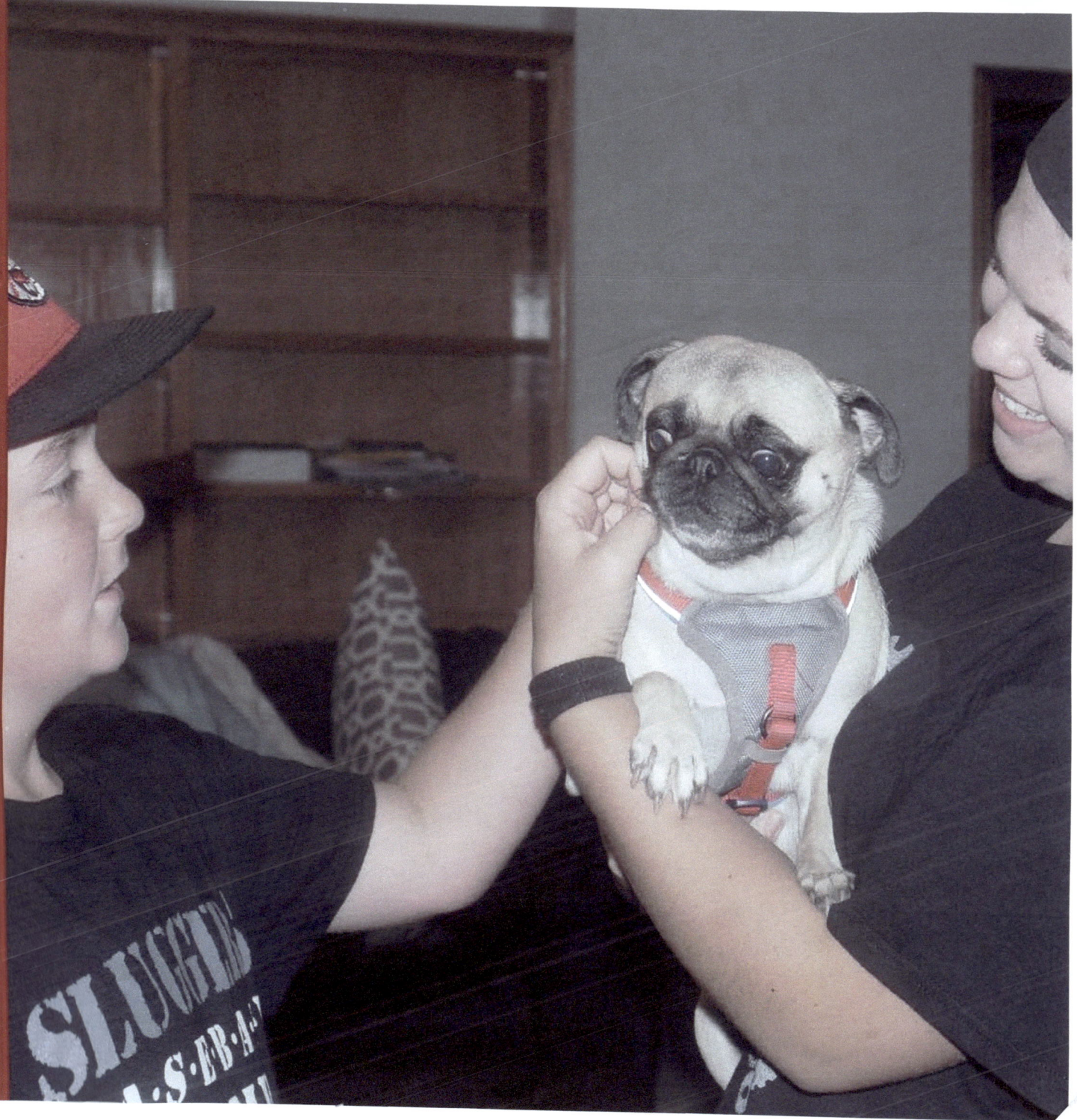

Vacations make us more creative and give us a chance to share ideas and thoughts with our families.

Do you like to tell your mom or dad when you come up with an idea that sounds fun??

Me (Molly) bonding with my Aunt Shannan (Shannan Lowe)

A vacation gives you cool stories you can remember and talk about.

Me (Molly) sitting by the fireplace at the lake house.

A
vacation
gives us a
chance to see
people we
haven't seen
in a while.

How often
do you see
your relatives?

Me (Molly) saying
hi to Kel (Kelly Johansen)

A vacation helps us develop skills we didn't know we had.

I got to do some hiking through the woods. Do you like to hike?

Me (Molly) walking down to the boat dock.

A vacation is a chance to perfect skills that we might've learned in the past.

Tristen and I are testing my life jacket to see if it works.

Me (Molly) and Tristen (Tristen Lowe) at the lake.

A
vacation
gives us a
sense of
accomplishment.

I'm proud of
myself because
I can swim in
the lake.

Have you taken
lessons and
learned to swim?

Me (Molly) swimming in the
lake with my new life jacket.

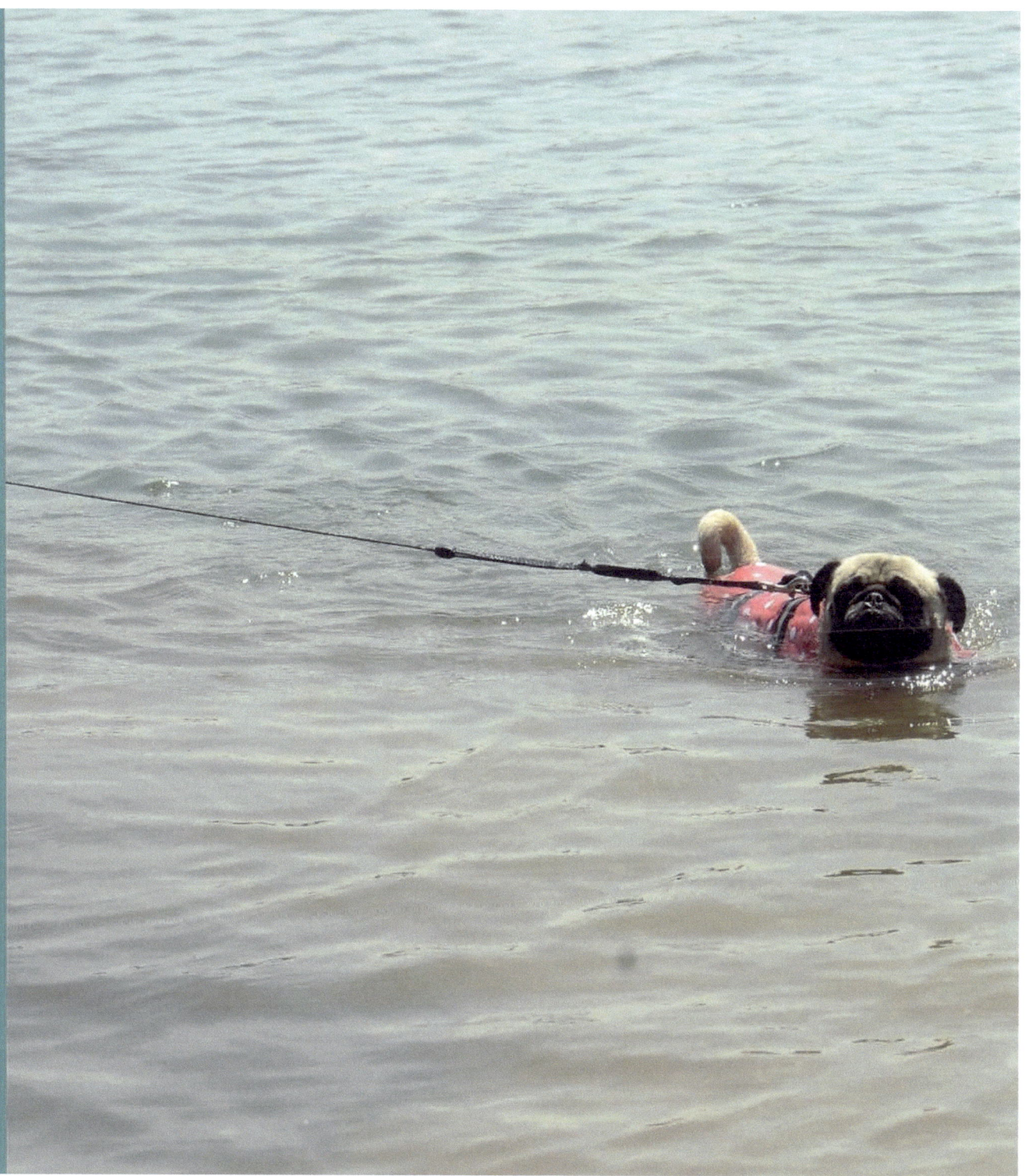

A
vacation
gives us
a chance
to be with
the people
we love.
I love my
boy. Who
do you love?

Me (Molly) floating
with my boy
(Jacob Johansen).

A
vacation
gives you
a chance
to try
something
new.

Can you find
me??

I had lots
of new
experiences
on vacation.

Do you
like trying
new things?

Me (Molly) on the boat
dock. Did you find me?

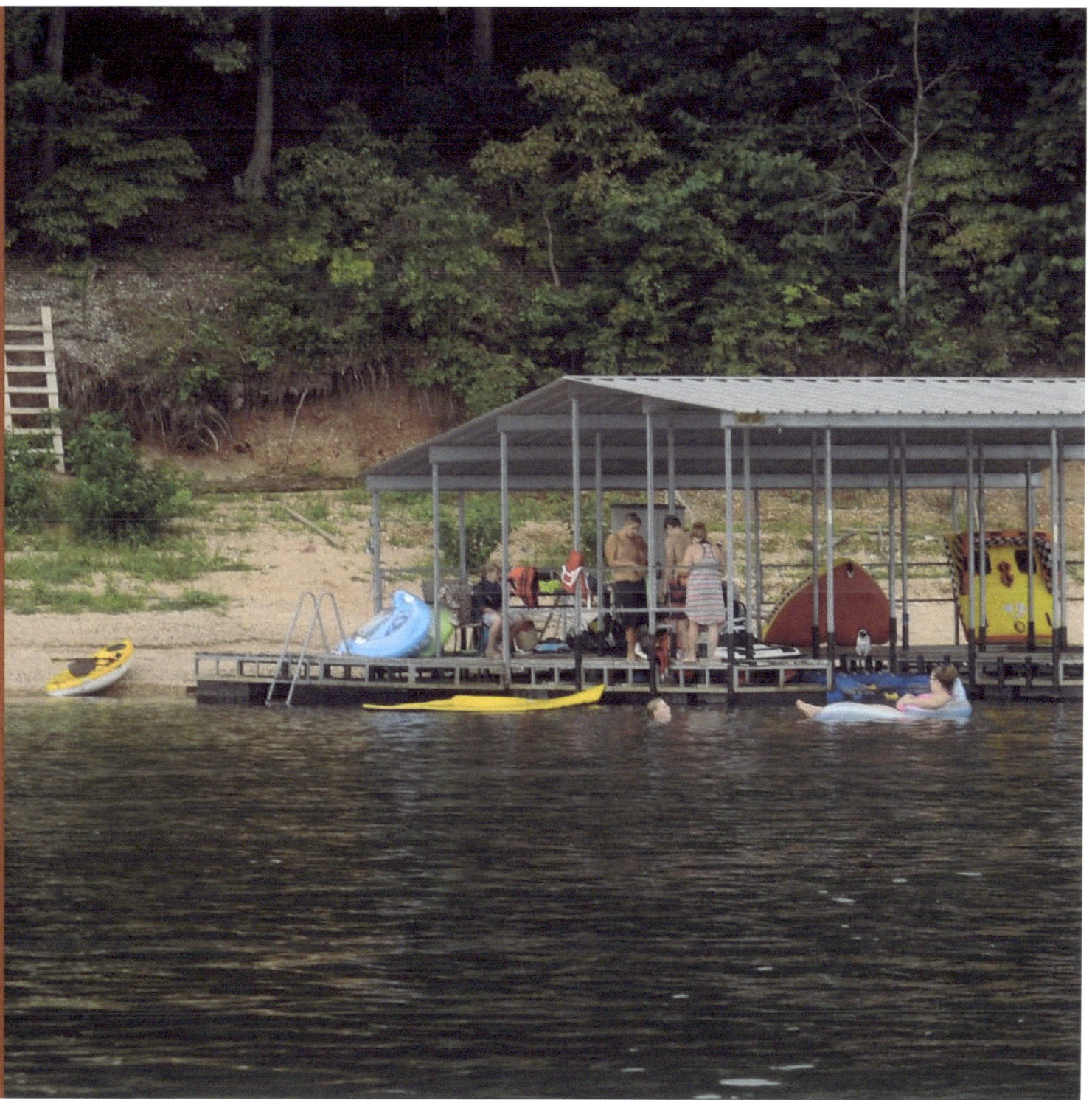

A vacation is a chance to do something exciting!!

This is a ski boat. It goes really fast and it's fun and exciting to ride in.

Me (Molly) and Uncle Rod (Rod Lowe) in his ski boat.

A
vacation
gives us an
opportunity
to make lots
of new
memories.

Have you
ever floated?
It's alot of
fun!!

Me (Molly) and Trevin
(Trevin Lowe) floating
on the lake.

A vacation gives us a chance to let other people help us learn a new skill.

I can swim but I've never swam in a lake.

Have you?

Danica Johnson making sure I (Molly) can swim in the lake.

Going on vacation relieves stress.

This is a pontoon boat. It goes slower than a ski boat but it's fun to ride in.

Have you ever ridden in a pontoon boat?

Me (Molly) and Uncle Rob (Rob Lowe) riding in the pontoon boat.

A vacation gives us a chance to relax and soak up some sun. I love lying in the sun. Do you?

Me (Molly) with my boy, Jacob (Jacob Johansen) and Kelly (Kelly Johansen).

A vacation gives us a chance to learn and enjoy new skills and activities.

I tried lots of new activities while in Arkansas.

You should try new activities when you go on vacation too.

Me (Molly) and Grandma Bev (Bev Stone) relaxing by the outdoor fire pit.

A vacation is a chance to sit down at the dinner table with our family and talk to them.

Do you eat with your family at a table?

Me (Molly) at the table that Uncle Rod built for the lake house.

A
vacation
helps you
learn
who you
really are.

We got to
see deer
walk
through
here
while on
vacation.

Have you
ever seen
a deer
up close?

Me (Molly)
relaxing in
the back yard.

A vacation is a chance to run around in your pajamas all day.

Do you have a favorite pair of pajamas?

Me (Molly) playing with Tristen (Tristen Lowe)

A vacation allows us to see the beauty around us.

I watched this sunrise with my mom. Have you ever watched a sunrise?

Me (Molly) watching the sunrise with mom as she is taking photos.

A vacation is a chance to rest, which gives us more energy.

We need to be on our best behavior during our vacations so our parents can relax too.

Me (Molly) relaxing on the deck.

A vacation helps you realize you have the support of your family, no matter how far apart you live.

Do you have relatives that live far from where you live?

Me (Molly) getting totally spoiled by Trevin (Trevin Lowe) and Ashley (Ashley Lowe).

A vacation helps you appreciate things at home that you may take for granted.

Have you ever roasted marshmallows in a fire pit?

Me (Molly) sitting by the outdoor fire pit on our vacation.

Going on vacation gives us a chance to learn about different cultures, food, history, geography, climate and environment.

Me (Molly) sitting by the lake house.

A
vacation
allows us to
experience new
sights and sounds.

Do you get
excited when
you see things
you haven't
seen before?

Me (Molly) walking along
the lake shore

Going on vacation gives us a sense of adventure.

This is my life jacket. Do you have one? Always remember to wear it around water.

Me (Molly) sitting in the kayak waiting for mom to give me a ride.

A vacation allows us to let our family know we love them.

I'm checking on my boy to make sure he's OK.

Do you ever worry about your mom or dad?

Me (Molly) watching my boy (Jacob Johansen) float.

A vacation gives us unexpected suprises.

Have you ever ridden on a jet ski?

Me (Molly) and Reed. (Reed Lowe)

A
vacation
gives
everyone
a chance
to act like
a kid again.

We all played
on this huge
yellow mat
at the lake.

Does it look
like fun??

Me (Molly) and Tristen
(Tristen Lowe) playing
on the yellow mat at the
lake.

A vacation gives us a chance to watch and enjoy someone else's skills.

He's good, isn't he?

Me (Molly) watching Reed (Reed Lowe) wakeboard.

A
vacation
gives us a
chance to be
outdoors and
enjoy the
weather.

Do you like
to be
outside?

Me (Molly) sitting on the
deck enjoying the sunshine.

A vacation makes time stand still and reminds us to thank the people that took us on vacation.

Me (Molly) watching a beautiful sunrise with my mom and my boy.

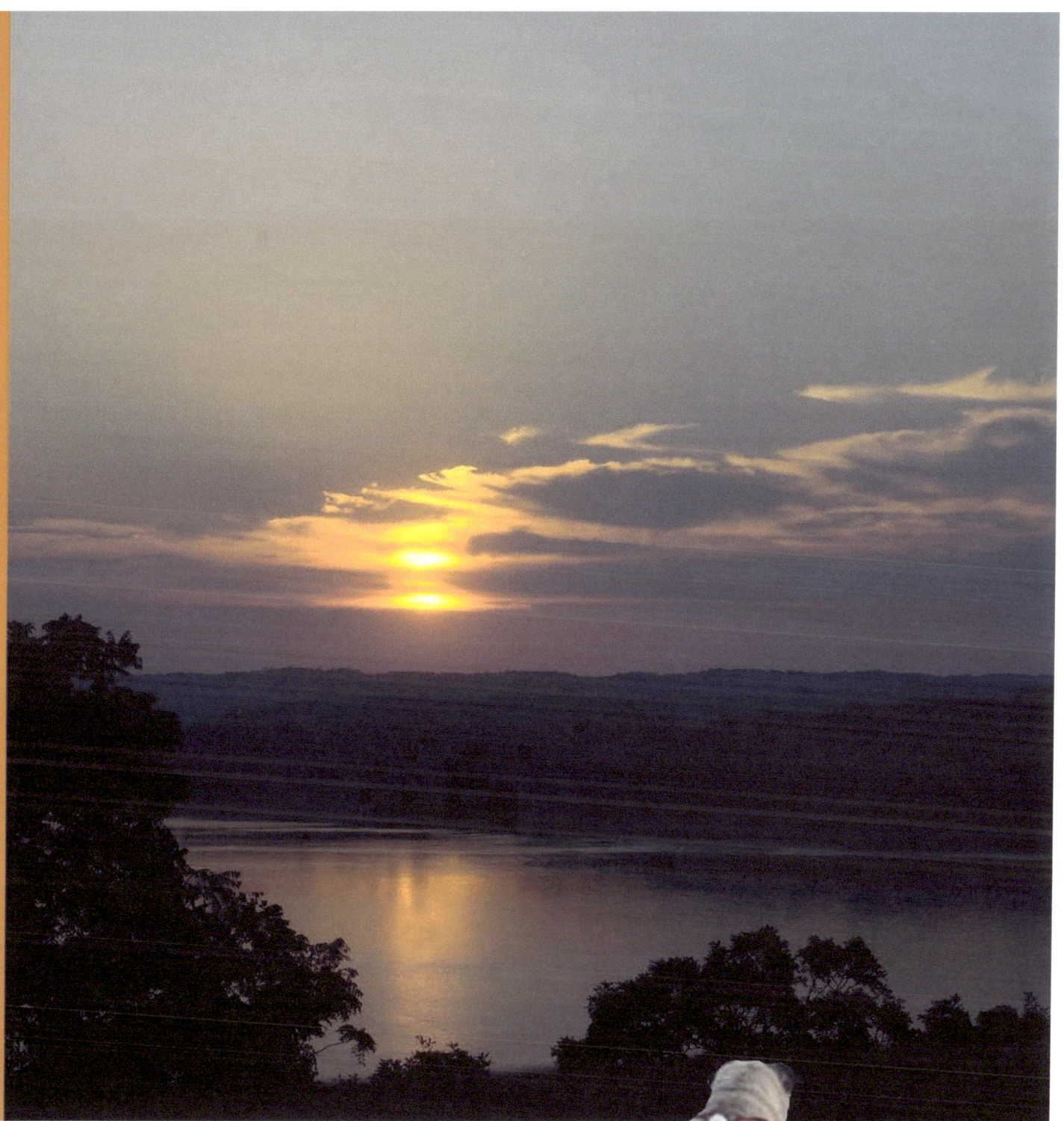

Taking a
yearly vacation
helps us to live
a longer life,
according to
scientists.

I hope you have
enjoyed vacationing
with me.

Me (Molly) and Grandma Bev
(Bev Stone) acting as the dock
patrols.

A vacation
might make
you want to
go home and
take a nap.
(ha. ha.)

That's what
happened to
me. I had so
much fun, I
wore myself
out!!

Me (Molly) on the couch
at home resting from my
vacation.

ABOUT MOLLY

Molly is a busy 4-year old pug that lives in Kansas. She stays busy as she helps her mom create these books. Her favorite thing to do is go to schools, libraries, and daycares and visit with the children after her mom reads Molly's books to them. When she's not working with her mom, she loves to go for walks at the park, eat her favorite treats, take baths, and play with her sister, Dolly.

www.ingramcontent.com/pod-product-compliance
Lightning Source LLC
Chambersburg PA
CBHW041000426
42448CB00002B/80